More praise for about:blank

'Words must be some kind of cybernetic hoax,' Adam Wyeth writes in this hallucinatory and shape-shifting collection. Musing on language and relationships, where 'words are looking through you', Wyeth conjures a seeking consciousness from the restless 'blanks' of our lives, and like W.S. Graham, a modernist romantic, Wyeth makes writing a raison d'être. The diversity and depth of these inquiries into poetic identity, and self-hood are by turn meditative and dramatic. Here's a book which delights in the 'drunkenness of things being various', and fuses connections from the inner and outer lives of its speakers. Imaginatively rhizomatic, about:blank is both a playful and deadly serious manifesto about how language shapes who we are or what we might be.

Paul Perry

Wyeth is a remarkable wordsmith with a truly distinctive and unique approach to the craft – in that his words play like firecrackers within their own sound and metaphor scape, truly blending poetic idioms with oblique narrative to produce a highly distinctive and evocative set of worlds unlike any other writer in the field today. about:blank takes readers on an epic journey through a dreamtime text of isolation, love, loss and misspent language that is contemporary Dublin. Written as a circular mixture of narrative-poetry, prose, monologue – the work has also been adapted as an immersive audio journey that is suspended within a binaural stereo soundscape. With the highly regarded and unique talents of actors Olwen Fouéré and Owen Roe this is certain to be a highly memorable, high-profile offering in these times of social isolation.

Michael Barker-Caven
Artistic Director, Civic Theatre, Dublin

Also by Adam Wyeth from Salmon Poetry

Poetry

Silent Music (2011)

The Art of Dying (2016)

Drama

This Is What Happened (2019)

Essays

The Hidden World of Poetry: Unravelling Celtic Mythology
in Contemporary Irish Poetry
Foreword by Paula Meehan (2013)

the arts council an chomhairle ealaíon | funding literature

salmonpoetry**40**
Celebrating 40 Years of Literary Publishing

Praise for SILENT MUSIC

The title poem of Adam Wyeth's remarkable debut collection starts with some newsy observation which, with a smooth change of gear, turns into a probing meditation, a moment of almost-illumination... Such marrying of wit with lyric grace, and the circumspect and patient crafting throughout, make these poems a pleasure to read, and re-read.

Maurice Riordan

Silent Music is a clever volume that playfully questions taken-for-granted certainties... a fresh and imaginative voice is evident.

Borbála Faragó *The Irish Times*

Silent Music is an impressive début collection which showcases the author's ability across a wide variety of short forms.

Dave Lordan *Southword Journal*

Praise for THE HIDDEN WORLD OF POETRY

Adam Wyeth is a gifted commentator/close reader. 'A hearer and heartener.'

Seamus Heaney

Wyeth is exactly the kind of reader poets dream of. Deeply intuitive, interested in everything to do with words. Pasternak remarked that each word comes to us carrying all its ghosts; Adam, as a learned and productive poet himself, respects those ghosts and understands the shamanic heft, the magic potential of each word, and the spell-like nature of a line of poetry.

Paula Meehan

Wyeth's essays excavate the intricate Celtic motifs running through his chosen poems with charm and precision. In doing so he performs the dual task of bringing less familiar work to the fore as well as illuminating new ways of reading old favourites.

Josephine Balmer

Praise for THE ART OF DYING

The Art of Dying *is divided into three sections, with each section demonstrating a different and gradually more daring poetic approach... this is a book which hold within it two more books; each decreasing in size but gradually containing more and more insights.*

Tara Bergin *Poetry North Review*

The Art of Dying *is a beautifully crafted performance by a poet who brings a cold, thoughtful eye to the eternal themes. The poems are alive with wit, long contemplation, and verbal energy.*

Michael O'Loughlin

There are fascinating and exciting things going on in Irish poetry at the moment. Adam Wyeth – who was named one of Poetry Ireland Review's *'Rising Generation' in 2016 – is at the heart of them. This outstanding collection deserves to be widely read.*

Ross Cogan *Orbis*

Praise for THIS IS WHAT HAPPENED

Civic Associate Artist playwright Adam Wyeth is a most accomplished, mature and distinctive voice in a time of declining craft. His work is highly textured, layered and in turn exciting and uncomfortable. This Is What Happened: A Triptych *is exactly this; a piece that pushes boundaries whilst delivering exceptional dramatic power and quality in production.*

Michael Barker-Caven Artist Director, Civic Theatre, Dublin

//about:blank]>,   pops   up   now and again:
}

      };

// a momentary hiatus before the required window opens.
     People get confused about why, = and what to do next.) {

</ about:blank is a starting point. >

    Everyone occasionally gets about:blank. If someone
      asked you to define 'blank', what would you say?
  < 0) {   'Nothing', I suppose.
      Maybe it would be easier for you if you saw
       it as a blank page.) {

<!-- That is exactly what about:blank is. -->

      }, As soon as you write, it stops being blank.
   I don't know what about:blank is. about:blank presents
alternatives.() {

<="I can't remember my first time finding about:blank.
    I was waylaid by it. One day about:blank just appeared,
      then it fragmented. I decided to get rid of
       about:blank. And typically, from wanting
     nothing, about:blank returned. -->

about:blank
adam wyeth

Published in 2021 by
Salmon Poetry
Cliffs of Moher, County Clare, Ireland
Website: www.salmonpoetry.com
Email: info@salmonpoetry.com
Copyright © Adam Wyeth, 2021

ISBN 978-1-915022-02-8

Cover image: Black Panther Eyes © Eric Gevaert | Dreamstime.com
Internal Images by Noelle Cooper

Cover Design & Typesetting: *Siobhán Hutson*

Printed in Ireland by Sprint Print

*Salmon Poetry gratefully acknowledges the support of
The Arts Council / An Chomhairle Ealaíon*

Contents

You do not need to leave your room. Remain sitting at your table and listen. Do not even listen, simply wait, be quiet, still and solitary. The world will freely offer itself to you to be unmasked, it has no choice, it will roll in ecstasy at your feet.

Franz Kafka

The struggle of literature is in fact a struggle to escape from the confines of language; it stretches out from the utmost limits of what can be said; what stirs literature is the call and attraction of what is not in the dictionary.

Italo Calvino

Some collaboration has to take place in the mind between the woman and the man before the art of creation can be accomplished. Some marriage of opposites has to be consummated.

Virginia Woolf

It is not the literal return to alchemy that is necessary but a restoration of the alchemical mode of imagining. For in that mode we restore matter to our speech—and that, after all, is our aim: the restoration of imaginative matter, not of literal alchemy.

James Hillman

Life has always seemed to me like a plant that lives on its rhizome. Its true life is invisible, hidden in the rhizome. The part that appears above ground lasts only a single summer. Then it withers away—an ephemeral apparition.

Carl Jung

The feminine will return. Across the seas Iseult is waiting. And when Iseult comes, the self-satisfied patriarchal world will never be the same.

Robert A. Johnson

We have kept our death secret to make our life possible.

Clarice Lispector

The image of death is the beginning of mythology.

Joseph Campbell

The stable state of a living organism is to be dead.

Norbert Weiner

HIRST

... And so I say to you, tender the dead as you would yourself be tendered, now, in what you would describe as your life.

He drinks.

BRIGGS

They're blank, mate, blank. The blank dead.

Silence.

HIRST

Nonsense.

Harold Pinter, from *No Man's Land*

Dedicated to all human beings

from *In Rainbows* Radiohead

Untitled

The woman in charge of the charity shop
says she's given birth to me.
All those years in my country
I was a gestating egg.

Now   here I am
limbs and crown
a recent émigré.

I lock up   and watch the shop
grow small   and dark.
I feel like a drone circling above
as someone thumbs the controls.

My whole life
*   could fall*
*   through their fingers*
*   in a matter*
of minutes.

I sink towards the city lights
tall buildings stick out like teeth.
An unbroken stream of people rush past.

*   I can't tell where we start or end.*
Does the stone fork the river
*   or the river fork the stone?*
There is a book in the shop

it stands on the shelf waiting
for eyes   to give it sight
and voice   to give it breath.

about:blank

Prologue

It's late –
I look out of the window onto Grosvenor Square
and catch the moon
behind the tree
a black cat watches across the street

I look out of the window
and see
a man   get into a car
no   he's stepping out
I look out of the man stepping out of a car
shutting the door
a comforting clunk
the whole car sleeps

the moon is scaling the tree

I pick up a pace
patting my pockets
then stop
under the tree
I return to the car
bleep it awake   open the door

I search for something
that stirs and rocks
with my weight
as I root through
the glove compartment

[there are no gloves in the glove compartment anymore
      all that's over]
I rummage down the side of the doors
      sliding my arms
down the back-pocket sleeves of the front seats

     what is it he's searching for

he's coming out
     he closes the door
     an equivocal clunk

did he find what he was looking for
     I don't see anything
on his person   in his hand

the black cat slinks across the street
the whole episode has become a mystery
and he doesn't know I know it exists

     but who else looks
who sees me looking now
     a stranger   looking over
     no   looking down

     a man about town ~~*a man about a woman*~~
a town about a woman
     who sees
not what I see but what I don't

the moon is free of the tree at last
and catches the cat's eye
      holding its tongue
who looks out of the man
      onto Grosvenor Square

the slate rooftops are moonwashed
the gardens sleep in their lost colours.

a woman
      is coming for me
as large as the city
      this is what happens
when we look out of the window
      all of the time
      everywhere
now   *in Dublin*

1

Summer's Death / Seed Fall

It happened that we were both together, I don't remember where.
It was the end of October. The days were thinning out.
I was walking the streets looking for Rosie, she's my cat.
I hadn't seen her for days.
All the colours of the world are revealed before they are about to die.

§

This is the way it is,
the way it always ends.
It comes back
to the one
who won't forget
the time it went
and returns
to the same moment.

§

Everything on repeat.

§

A woman on a bench told me to take a seat.
She was eating a sandwich and offered me half.
I refused of course. She told me she once had a dog.
I should say I told her first I had a cat. She told me
her dog, Oscar, was a pure pedigree of some kind.
He wandered the streets at night too. But she
never worried, she knew it was part of his nature

and also that Oscar would come back as she had
the best bacon. That was her secret weapon.
All dogs love bacon, like all men, she said.

§

The hum of the city   swirls   in the wind
as the leathery leaves   tussle   with the ground
offering themselves   up   to the footpath.

§

                                                    Final windfalls.

§

What happened is this –
        we both got twisted
        in conversation,
and I came around to the realisation
that her Alsatian   Oscar
sounded very much like a person
        I used to know.

I looked at my watch,
time had gone slow.
Everything on repeat.

I pictured Rosie stalking a bird,
or stock-still on a wall

under a willow,
hypnotized by light   through leaves,
passing up the urge   to pounce.

§

The low sun turns treetops into stained-glass mosaics.

§

This is the way it is.

§

It begins with a memory.

It begins with a seed.

It does not begin as it means to go on.

It grows up. Stretches in the sun.

It recoils from shadows. It sways in the wind.

It greets the moon with a face like a coin.

It has seen it all before.

It has never seen anything before.

Everything is first time.

A blank mind. Unwashed. Purity.

No smell. New sheets. Spring. Lambing.

No blood. A vitreous eyeball.

It cracks out of the carapace.

It cuts through.

This is the violence.

It opens its head.

Branches appear.

§

There is something else
                    underlying
                    everything between
                    this woman and myself.
What that something
                    else is
                    eludes us
                    in its small furriness.
It comes out for a minute and I mark it.
                                    I think I might
                                    enjoy this more
                                    than anything.
It is the thought of Rosie I love,
                    that she's out there
                    somewhere prowling
                    the stygian streets.
I feel like a bird pecking at a nut,
                            knowing
                            there's something
                            greater looking over.

It comes back to the one who loves
               too much
               and can't forget
               the time it went.

§

          I've been dithering in the dark all my life
          cooped up in a womb.
I used to read ▮▮▮▮ and these words
meant something to me,
now the words ▮▮▮▮ *shudder*
in a frozen monitor
stuck in the betweentime
          of a loading webpage.
The about:blank ▮▮▮▮ in the chest,
its cut in the throat   a stick
          between stones
                    holding up the dearly beloved.

§

she closes her eyes
we are all in the dark
rivers ▮▮▮▮ canals ▮▮▮▮ coastlines
the whole city looking ▮▮▮▮ the other way.
She sleeps in me as I sleep in her

I will be this city one day

and then I'll be let back

into the black of her.

§

This is the way it is, the way it always begins.
The woman on the bench had enough
of my prattle and she rattled off with her trolley
of belongings, murmuring sweet nothings
to the pigeons. We can speak of a voice
between us, we can think of a massive gap,
we can imagine a tunnel with my cat on a mat
at one end and me at the other, it never
adds up to anything but itself. I'm on a bench
thinking of this, watching the woman
with the trolley become a blurring distance.
Yet I know I'm doing nothing of the sort,
I'm somewhere else entirely, flying above
all this prittle-prattle, meridian of thought.

§

                                                    In every body
                                                out of each mouth.

§

This is   the way it is.
        The truth...   the lies...
The days...   the nights
            will cloy to our f l i m s y   l i
                                                    v
                                                      e
                                                        s.

§

Another   life   we know nothing about.
A furball that builds in the stomach forms a guttural in the throat,
                                    and falters into the blank.

§

Each life hides   another life inside
another voice   never heard out loud
speaks in its own way   a silent film
unfolding   an unbroken story
of loss   this voice ripples
in each of us
call it   the INTERNAL FEMININE
she lies curled   like a question mark
in bed   or dare I say snake
a woman   in foetal position
coiled   like a brand-new fern
about to open   she is bereft
smelling the shirts   of someone who left
is it her father   her brother her lover
let's call it   the FORSAKEN MASCULINE
the disappearance of one whose voice is heard
in a dog's bark   or at least felt in the harsh
October bite   the dank nights that grow longer
each passing year   he walks with the secret voice
in his back pocket   it moves through him
he locks the car door   and gets closer with every step
and every moment   is a step inside him
that makes it move   further away
he keeps walking   until one day he falls
into his own shadow   and no one can see it and no
one can hear it and   no one can touch it and no
one can smell it   and no one can taste it

the secret   walks on never giving itself away

§

where did it go

        split asunder
        by the shadow that grows
                        like a gulf
an oil-spill   mushrooming
seeping into everything.
Let's not make light of what can't be seen precisely.
            Let's not lose pursuit   of specifics
                        on the grounds of reality
destroyed after last year's storm
                        they are waiting to be born
new ferns unfurl   fanning the earth.

§

                        This is the way   the way always.

§

I'm on a beach near Irishtown. There are people swimming all around. She
                        has just gone to the café to get drinks.
    I'm lying on my back being lulled by the sound of waves and children
                        playing. The sun is beating down.
    I feel I haven't had a life yet, that I've just been dropped from space into
                        this place. Everything begins now.
    I look at the sky and realise I can't move, I am paralysed by this thought.
            The wind blows grains of sand on my face.

Everything I've known before is washed away. I realise everything that I
thought I was,
is just the surface, and that what is true is blank.

§

I am not who I am.

§

Voices at the back of a room   everyone speaking over one another
I can't make out   who is saying what.
For a moment   I have a picture of myself   in another skin.

A figure bends down   and hands me a cold drink.
I lift my arm towards it,   Adam   reaching for God
in the Sistine Chapel   as if all life depended   on this fizz

The sounds   of children and waves return   shifting towards me   from another
world   and she talks about the price of drinks. I nod and listen and think   I
cannot see the sand that lies beneath...
At the same time, I'm half-listening to strangers.

§

Sometimes I wonder   if all communication   isn't fantasy.

§

Each word creates
another universe
out of the one before

which in turn creates
other words
that are not words

and they occur
as it were
in their own worlds

independent of thought
insouciant
to the back room chatter

where insolvent smiles
while away the small hours.

Words must be some kind of cybernetic hoax
to try and coax   a confession out of

     dipping in and out of the mind
a black box switch   in which
we are duped   by their respected sounding

a circular relationship that engenders change
     in the environment
and that alteration is reflected in the system
in some manner
     triggering a structural transformation.

Landing upon a word   is a love transferred
Alighting from a word   sparks pairs of opposites

§

Think of two people talking politics,
poles apart in their views.

Take that word:
                    pole
they are both either end of this
                          pole
they are both grasping at the same
                              pole
in the end there's no difference because
they are talking about the same
                          pole
in different ways but neither one of them
can hear the other because the
                    pole
is so long that you have to shout to be heard
and when you have to shout to be heard
you can only hear your own voice.

What you have are two transmitters and no receiver.
To receive, you have to empty yourself,
but you can't be empty
          if you're full of static fury.

What I'm getting at,
          or attempting to suggest,
          is that I'm aware
as I propose
          this particular episode
                    of this particular life,
on this particular day,
there is no way
          you're going to grasp
          what I first imagined,
and second   set out to express.

Yet in this flight of fancy
      what you suppose will be what happens,
(and as I give voice to this particular life
      another life grows inside).
Not that anything is supposed to happen
not that   anything can   happen.
What is forming   has already
      been   formed.
What is happening   is as
      stillborn
and as stock-still
      as the gaps   between   these   words.

§

A white   field   of   blank.

§§

        There is nothing more to see and nothing more to say.

§

Nothing more, say, than seeing a woman through a window

on a bus. You attach to that glimpse whatever it is you
are open to now. Most people don't see this particular person

on this particular bus, but this one person does.
And that is what this story – if I can call it a story – which I won't

– is about.

What does this glimpse tell us about ourselves?

It tells us what we want to hear. It tells us we are on the bus, having been glimpsed by someone on the street.

There may be a faint picture within you now and yet I have not mentioned any distinctive details.

They don't even exist, which is a crazy proposition, because we know very well, or did, that two strangers, a passer-by and a passenger are always with us.

The glimpse passes in a second, but the thought attached to that glimpse lingers and leads to something else, something hidden that must come out.

An essence.

This is what the momentary chimera is about.

It is for you to seek out the truth of the passer-by and the passenger and to decide whether any part of them is worth detaining.

If we call the passenger Claire, the passer-by Stephen, we add fuel to the fire of hallucination.

These schoolbook names that stretch throughout the English-speaking world and beyond resonate with certain reflexes.

We know damn well what is happening here.

Well, *we* have no idea actually, but it's all about that slippery pole again.

Everything before and after sex is exactly what it suggests; everything between is where and what literature takes off.

I do hope you don't think I'm fiddling you, what I have to say is wholly serious. In the words of a great sage –

You have to split the stick to find the light.

§

By communicating with the dream we are able to glean its meaning.

§

                                        This is everything that forgets.

§

Stephen sees her face again through the glass. He recalls each feature
rippling under the reflected shades of the shops and houses;
the snailing traffic   fracturing   her mouth   and jawline
into broken shards.   A stained glass puzzle.
He buys a pen and pad in Spar and sits by the Grand Canal.
The words are tentative at first, the descriptions vague and disjointed. He's
following the darts of thinking and the words are helping him to ground
his thoughts into what feels, to him at least, like a fully-fixed certainty.

§

A gabbling
gang of students
released from

the Atlas Language
School behind him;
a steady succession

of vernaculars
making love
individually:

wrangling
                    mangling,
disentangling   tongues
jostling for elbowroom –

leaning towers
        of babel by
                    the water's edge.

§

Stephen's best image is Claire's face
reflected in the glass.

The exact words escape him.

They escape me.
She escapes us all.

But a latent power remains

beneath this sideways rush;
an impression

of condensation on glass,

her face
a new penny in a fountain

looking out from the dark.

§

A penny if any, for where do they go?
Our thoughts like old water continue to stir.

§

Penny is the wrong currency. Obviously.
Stephen's holding out for silver, but
he may just get away with its shadowy
glimmer; the idea of coins and Lady Luck
is enough to go on. Indistinct instincts.
There is no going back from here.
He types it up at home and discovers
the suddenness of a clear-cut verb,
the satisfaction of an adjective's swerve.
He finds a melodic coherence, a precision
and elegance he has never known previously.

§

Out of the love never encountered: an invisible stranger.

§

Where is Claire now?

Is she, at any level, aware her image has been played over and again, in Stephen's head?

She might sense something.

She is known to daydream, especially on the ride home under the plane trees that flank the South Circular.

For all we know, Claire caught sight of Stephen, her eyes meeting his behind the glassy sheen for a second between wondering what to have for tea and who was around for the weekend.

Perhaps the glimpse was just enough for her to think about a boy she knew from home.

Whatever happened to him, she wonders, as she passes Dolphin's Barn and moves on to Rialto.

An older voice behind her says: *'They' are taking over!*

§

Claire's aware that naming is caging.
          Something seen is something taken.
The living, sacrificed in dead words,
          trapping a cosmos into an hour glass.
The more that we write the more we forget.
What remains of the living breathes in the dead.
          Would the English, for example,
have taken any other *native* tree as a national symbol
if its name were not linked to 'druid'?

§

What are feelings, then,

before their sounding,

and what are feelings when

they are unspoken?

Has language altered our reality

so much

that we move in a hall of mirrors,

projecting

skewed images

onto the world

and only seeing

what is thrown back at us?

§

Claire's wary when it comes to the hallucination of conversation.
She has a good inner-ear for what's really being said
            behind the thread of words.
While we have uncovered the slippery nature of language –
            that words
don't always mean what they say,
            or put another way,
            the speaker invariably
            remains in the shadows
            of what they're saying
            and it's more about the current and humming between –
Claire's aware
            of the generative properties
            words embody

the esoteric incantations
locked in a series of letters   which in the right order

can transform reality   unearthing a language
within the language   a molecular pattern
of circular causal wires   springing from a level
below meaning   carried by the land.

Some people have an innate ability to separate the dross from people's sounds,
others can't tell the mole from the mound.

§

                   Claire discerns another language:
                           a language of the earth.

§

As she alighted the bus

Claire walked home
with a prickling feeling
that the state of the world
didn't just apply

to the woman on the bus

but that it applied to her
and not just to her,
but to us.

(The slippery pole again.)

Although Claire
could guess
what the woman meant
by *'They' are taking over,*
the words took her somewhere else –

deeper,
darker,
coiling
inside her,

  a slithery, inky blank.

Claire knew then
her life was not her own:
she was in someone else's hands,
being shaped in ways
she could not control.

§

An image erased yet somehow known.
This is the way of no return.

§

The thought passed in a minute, but it was enough for Claire to feel a rush
of sickness as she blinked and came back to her life in Rialto.

§

Earlier in the day Claire had been to Dublin Zoo.
She liked to go in early spring –
  crocus time,
  trees in bloom.
She saw herself in all the animals.

Believed each animal was
        a totem,
        a talisman.
This, it should be said, was more an instinctive
sensation than anything pushing its way into words.
        But Claire,
        being Claire,
couldn't help but wonder
about her own limits.

She enjoyed the lions,
        the meerkats,
        the pandas,
but most of all, Claire loved watching

§

The Black Panther

§

The cage looked empty but then

two amber eyes loomed out,
followed by blue-black fur,

a full, muscular profile

materialized: **Pure Cat** –
for once, an irrefutable fact,

it sloped towards Claire

sniffing the air around her,
sidling from left to right,

holding her eyes.

She tried to imagine
what it might be thinking.

Nothing human,

how could it? Every inch of it
exhibited burning instinct:

thick panting blankness bore into her.

§

Those were her thoughts while she watched the panther's blue-black paws
pad back into the shadows. Then the cat roared and her reverie was ended.
    That was that.
    Going, she caught his sweet, honeysuckle scent.

§

Within the love that never meets, the animal is released.

§

I don't think a cage is necessarily a bad place.

We can spend our whole life
cocooned in one enclosure.

All those coats in the closet.

My fear is that I'll only be going
from one womb to another.

§

This is the way through.

§

Stephen was Googling where to publish when he came across a free workshop taking place in Rathmines. He sped down Leinster Road with the Claire poem in his pocket. He wondered if this was the beginning of something. Stephen, the poet.

A gust of wind swirled up some litter and leaves and Stephen reeled off his lines through their circular dance. He loved the way certain ones rubbed up against one another, sliding off at the tongue.

The poetry workshop took place in a private room in the old library. Stephen's poem, like everyone's, was read in silence. He noticed the others jotting marks on their copies, circling certain words, scratching out others, writing comments in the margins.

As Stephen read aloud he wondered which of the words the group would pick out; his voice grew smaller and smaller disappearing inside that inside-tunnel. One by one, each person offered their penny's worth.

Stephen sank deeper into his chair as he saw Claire's image defiled in front of him. Not a single line remained intact. The sheets were collected and delivered back; a stillbirth swaddled in white cloth.

Claire, or at least, Claire's face in the pane, had vanished. Stephen walked to Portobello Bridge and dropped the tatters of his battered poem in the canal. All his watery letters bled into one vanishing word.

§

A blinding blank.

§

Of course, Claire
wasn't dead, because Claire
doesn't exist. But Claire
of course does very much exist. There are Claires
present everywhere, each one brings their own unique Claire-
ness to this particular individual. There is nothing Claire
does not contain. Since her defacement on the page, Claire's
image has almost completely disappeared

from Stephen,
who himself is now so far removed
that he's as pointless as a paper bag
                blowing down
                Rathmines Road.

§

Claire was on her way back from the corner shop: she had bought a loaf of bread and a carton of milk. As she walked, she could feel a slight shadow trailing her. She shrugged off this vague sensation, but the shadow continued to grow around her.

§

Each lane articulates another voice.
Each voice gets tangled
down another back alley, which leads
to a derelict building:
a boarded-up door
standing dumb without question,
the smashed eyes of a seer
either side, peering through.
A stone slab sleeps
in the navel of the basement
waiting to be opened.
Claire herself might as well
be blind as she senses this place
assumingly.

§

No such thing as the truest sense.

§

One man
in the window
is cut in two.
What are you
to do
with this sum?
Is the man
reduced
to fifty per cent

because of his
position
according to you
or is he actually
cut up?
A split stick.

§

Who is the one
beyond the city
beyond the man
and the woman
divided by the city?

§

The myth before the myth.

§

This is the way back to the one with both hands on the wheel driving through the night, slipping like silk between streetlights. Hands firm at 9 & 3, slinking down avenues, creamily, in a dream, purring smooth as a black cat lapping up the night. He's got the whole world in his hands.

The steering wheel stands for the heavens. The wheel of control: the wheel of fortune, the star wheel, the zodiac, the pre-Christian sun wheel, the Round Table, the mandala. The star of the show holds the universal in their hands. She's got you and me brother in her hands.

Before the cross was a cross it was a disk. We took the great wheel out of the sky. The feminine circle made invisible, sacrificed on the cross. He takes the wheel of her life into his own hands. The invisible heavens wheel above as they steer a steady course beyond that bounding rim of the wheel of becoming.

The power of the engine, a thousand horses. A ravenous beast roaring from the east eats up the miles, unravelling the white ribbon road. Headlights, ghost trails chasing the dark knight of the soul. The only thing between is the scenery, made abstract by satnav. Everything they need to see within is neon-lit in the leather interior.

He, who pierces through the valley – now just a langue of digital signs, he who once worshipped the wheel now holds it daily: rootless, ahistorical. This is life, this capsule, this cocoon, until it splits open its husk.

§

A car is
not a car,
it is a
symbol
for the
trans-
migration
of souls
entering
the
celestial
city,
through
a cat's eye.

§

A car is
a woman
stopped
on the road
that a man
has just
stepped
out of
who is
a cat
waiting
to jump
who is a
beggar
asking
for change
from a
child
who is
a bird
falling.

§

Our concern is with the woman walking through
Rialto
who is already falling. It is the Claire within the
Claire
prompting the whole debacle. Here we fall back
into
the historical ego of tribes, our fathers and
mothers.
Can they be left at the door like a pair of
outworn
shoes after we've tripped down the sweet-smelling
avenue?

Can you close the door on the person who brought
you
to the threshold in the first place? The movement from
one
side of the mind to the other, from the
bottom
of the body to the top, from the quotidian
purchase
of milk and bread at the corner shop to a
supraconsciousness?

§

                                        Paper bags: poetry.

§

She's in love with a poet who doesn't have a face.
They move along the path and a shaft of light cuts
between branches. She's in love with a poet who
doesn't have a voice. The thrust of their words moves
beneath their feet, kicked-up leaves, a quiver
of light just out of sight, a cloud on the horizon,
a ribbon of wind begins to hint at what cannot be known.

She's in love with a poet she'll never hold.
Lost looks take place in another room that cannot be
entered; the suggestion of certain features represent
the whole, something to do with SYNECDOCHE.
A locked door without a key: a mouth without a tongue.
Doors that will never open on their own; water in a lock.
She's in love with a poet of remembrance,

a certain embrace, the way legs twist under chairs,
and hands slip beneath, brushing knees. She's in love
with a poet who's a long time dead. A hole in the head
opens. Lines uncoil as the morning light creeps along
the page; the dead poet's words blossom in her mouth.
She's in love with an unheard song. When poetry
is poetry nothing is said; it's nature itself keeping watch.

The eye of the storm listens in on a language unfound;
severed tongues buried in pockets of humus.
The looks are feminine, the sounds masculine.
The coming together of two primal forces
breaks the binary into multiple voices.
Behind the blind the fly sizzles in its own demise
becoming an extinguished wish.

Black birds flit from tree to tree.

§

She's in love with the first idea
last seen in the animal's eye.

§

As soon as Claire arrived home she took a shower.

Great thoughts come to us in the shower.
As we remove the layers and armour of our day,

our mind steps into its own private time and space.

But Claire's thoughts were not great or at least anything
substantial, rather she felt her small daydreams scatter

with the streams of water sluicing

over her face and glissading down her breasts,
slipstreaming around limbs,

south-circling the small of her back.

Afterwards, she floated vaguely out of the shower
like a child's pale balloon in a fog.

Her drip-dreaming figure reached for a towel

from the back of the door and she glimpsed
her smudged corporal blur in the mirror amid the teal tiles.

She wiped the mirror and looked at her face

in the watery reflection – bright as a new penny in the glass
that quickly started steaming over again.

She could have floated away, she thought.

Bathed in lightness, bathed in heat.
Steam was evaporating and soon

she would see herself clearer in the mirror.

Lightheaded, Claire then realised she had lost all sensation
of her body. The contours of her face started to blur

and the teal tiles became dark and the bathroom

began whirling all about her. She felt herself being
lowered down a deep well. She held on to the sink,

but her feet gave way.

Her knees buckled and thudded onto the tiles, followed
by her hips, elbows and finally her head smacking

like a husk to the floor.

Her eyelids started to flutter and she thought she could see
in the doorway a dark figure standing over her,

a big black bundle of fur with a tail, ready to take her.

Or was it just a towel hanging on the door?
Her mind raced back and she recalled

the bus ride home,

she caught someone looking at her from the street;
the bus, stopped. Two eyes the other side of the glass

like headlights, puzzled her out.

They shone into the back of her mind, just as her gaze
had entered earlier that day into the panther's cage,

dead in the centre of its black pupils.

Its gaze now her gaze, totally dark and expressionless.
Sucked into the other side. A computer

wiped clean of its data.

A room with not a stick of furniture. A coin face-down
at the bottom of a well. Her darkness complete.

An infinite blank.±

~~****Verbose Mode   Start up<   optimistic=~~
~~Warning{~~
~~   too many couples being created\~~

~~Chain mask: mismatch/   Darwin bootstrapper<~~

~~Optimistic DAD-~~   ~~Couldn't block sleep`~~

~~Legacy slip>~~   ~~Unsupported/ client/~~   ~~terminate~~

~~Channel changed+~~   ~~Promiscuous mode made~~

~~boot immediately] reboot~~
               ~~Hash free%~~

~~Warning EFI\clover~~   ~~Fip post integrity*~~
          ~~Found~~   ~~text////~~ ~~Free cache~~
~~Journal reply done/^***~~

§§§

I'm not going to lie
        and say
it never happened
or that it happened
        just as I say

This is
        the way it is

whatever happens
is   always questionable

The way   it always ends

        I could say   for instance
there was I   sitting by the banks
disturbing   the calm surface
        with a stick
        setting ripples
        within the reflection

It comes back

I could say   perhaps
I got   the wrong end
of the stick
         or in fact
the stick itself
had no end
         so then
         it was not a stick
I was holding   after all

The one who won't recall

what's in front of us   may be
something else   entirely

Everything on repeat

but there it is
the longer
I held it
         inside
the more I thought
it might   never
have happened

The way of no return

just because
something happens
doesn't mean
you   talk about it

The same moment

if you don't talk
about it
who's to say
          it happened
in the first place

§

This
is
the
way

way
leads
on to
way

§

But something did happen and is happening now.

§

Something happened   and can never be taken back
and in its happening   it continues to happen
and in its continuing   to happen is taken back to
the same point before   it happened and in that state
before happening   nothing is happening
at one and the same   time as it happens again

but this is not
which goes back to
in first happening
in always happening
in the way it first happened
it first happened another
so that every time
as it did before in the way
in an infinite number
disruptive happens
something always happens
and in never happening

what happened
when it first happened
it will always happen
it will never happen again
and in it not happening the way
happening happens another way
it happens it never happens
consecutive happenings happen
of ways in the way say something
giving birth to something else
and never happens at the same time
happens once and for all.

§

It comes back to the one who won't forget.

§

I once heard a story of a nameless boy
who   woke up dead.

Passages from a novel you can never forget.
Each word lodged   somewhere. A backroom.
A plangent refrain

played out   in a cello's strain.
A memory of birth.
How could we ever forget?   I never forgot.
It was stored,
kept safe for a rainy day.
Now all the days appear together
slooshing with leaves and twigs
down gutters and drains.

Watch then the moment it comes.
The roads are rivers,
pavements, mud banks.
Never the same pain twice.
The onlooker changes what's looked upon.
Don't look at me   that way.
I know what you're thinking
but you don't know what it's been like
to carry   this.
The failed anchor with its long drag.
The dead weight.
The slower it moves   the more pronounced.
Watch then   the moment it comes.
The truth is the sea's always been with us.
The ocean is not at the end but underneath everything.
And behind everything
the unseen, unbidden, unweeded lawns.
A door off its hinges.   Open space.

§

It comes from itself   a suffocating blank

§

It comes for Itself.

§

After the fire
new shoots
appear

in the   undergrowth
          and grow
to be as great
          as the trees
          they replace

and the forest's life
becomes part
          of a greater
          biodiversity
which knows
there is a fire
that will clear
          everything
          away
that happened

and in that
          the fire
continues to happen
until

the next fire
          takes its place

and the next fire
is the first
fire

and all the fires
          happening
at once
are the same fire

so when it comes
to saying something
          say

something new
        all we can say
is something happened

something
happened

and
can
never

be
taken
back.

§

This is the way it started with a knot in the gut and travelled up the torso
                    filling the lungs
and mushroomed into a sound   at the back of the throat, the tip
              of the tongue
unfurled at the birth canal lock   of the teeth and the lips blew
          out a flower.
Does it disappear in the shadow   or can it go on? Can it imagine
          something else
beyond its happening? Or does   it emerge in the flower as our future
        which is yet unnamed?

§

                            Arise and disappear.

§

I never told you about what lay beneath, did I? While waiting by the water
I felt myself being lowered into this weird architecture.
Call it a sunken ship sitting in silt with silver fish streaming through its
empty cabins. Only the silver could not be seen, as it's so dark down there.
This boat sits at the bottom and thanks to its shape things have to move
around it.
I call it the Moses-motion.
The sunken ship reminded me of a man next door I used to know,
I say know, I only knew him to look at, which I did on rare occasions
when I dared to peep over the hedge.
He had a front tooth missing and whenever he spoke he whistled slightly,
so that every word had an undertone both between and within it.

§

This is the way the pane of glass between
the beloved and the lover is removed.

§

I came to a bridge
              over a body   of water
I sat down on a bench   by the bank
        and ate   my sandwich
        the distant sound   of a tin-whistle
tickling   my ear
        the breeze   streaming
        through the willows   a frozen
fountain   of flickering leaves
a girl in a crop   top   lying   underneath
twisting the lead   of her headphones   round her
finger
tapping her feet
        her other hand   drawing

an invisible circle
around
her belly
      a silent beat
the shaking tree   to my right
talking in hushed tones   under the breeze
      its elephant's hide   pushing
up   against the sky
the shadow-branches
dancing on her skin
are a map of the city
the laidback canal   reflecting
whatever's thrown at it
pedestrians   cyclists   bridges   trees   you / me
      ... a dotted line of sleeping bags and tents   flap
along the bank   Ireland's new flag
all the way to Google's   glass façade
a mute swan
glides by
disturbing
the water's surface
before returning back   to the pellucid mirror
as if it had never been
      the closer we look
      the less
      we can distinguish
      between surface
      and reflections
thoughts floating   among images
second by second
then getting caught in the weeds
an isolated thought
rises   as a fish
into an idea
      before
disappearing
in a blank blur
below.

§

When the fisher king eats too soon
he suffers a mortal wound.

§

The tin-whistle becoming silent.
Everything still by the water.

Up is like down when ▮▬ .

Some people want to fill in the blank here,
others want to keep it as is.

I'm just throwing crumbs

for the pigeons and watching them
peck at my feet,

or setting a black cat among them.

§

Another swan sailed by, this time, a flag of peace.

§

An elderly woman sat beside me.

I told her my name but we didn't
share the same language. I leaned over

and could see her body

rippling out of the weeded bank, her sad
face reflecting a smile. She held

a compact in her hand

as if it were her own life. Something
was exchanged in the water.

Her features refined

and redefined by each undulation,
before settling back. Her body, an old map,

contained in a glass cabinet

through which no words could penetrate.
All her treasures locked safe inside.

She opened her mouth

and a shoal of tiny fish poured out.
I was about to respond

when a team of terns descended,

taking the breadcrumbs from my mouth
then flying off like messengers,

passing it on to their young.

§

Do not think you are lost. You are the water and earth that binds us.

§

It comes back.
This is the way.

§§§§

She returns some nights

when the streets are empty,
when the moon rises,

I look for her,

even though I'm aware
she's not there.

I imagine her still,
I imagine her now.

My little dark rose.

§

Rosie died two years ago.   Was she a cat?
        She drowned in the lock.
        Her soddenbodycaught   in the weeds
        of the bank.   I'm not denying   it happened
        I'm simply   looking   at something else.
        The same moment.

§

At the bottom of the water

where the dead depart she bears
the weight of a human heart.

An ancient moon-god

of the city. The heart of the system
is master of the word, the magic

of resurrection sails across the night

greets the dawn which roars
on the horizon, licks up the land

with its gold tongue,

swallowing the womb. The heart and
the tongue are one in every body

out of each mouth, all beasts,

all crawling things. Immanent
and transcendent.

§

When the eyes see,

the ears hear,

the nose breathes,

the mouth repeats

thoughts of the heart.

§

The world is looking through you.

§

The ground gives way beneath

it is a river

the skin of the water is not a mirror

it is a door

our unspoken thoughts linger here

I wade through

falling into the depths and layers of being.

Somewhere here I signed my name

I gave myself away to the night.

The dead leaves are blank tokens.

I forget what was said

but it must be deep and dank.

I place a leaf on my tongue and listen.

How is a child to know

what they are to forgo in the wood?

A child wounded by the word

which only the word alone can cure.

Disconnection is the tale

and the tail –

what we say

and what follows.

§

A split stick   breaks   into bud.

§

I am trying to come to terms
with who I am not.
I am standing in the dark hole
shivering.

The space all around goes on forever.
I find a voice
and follow it through the tunnel,
under the earth,

beyond language, there is a final door
that does not open
but can be entered
when the ur-word leaves the tongue

§

                                    the image and body are one.

§

Keep looking at the outside world until the outside world is no longer outside.

§

It's amazing to think when you see a tree that all of that came from a single seed.

        There, I said it.

Take this tree; doesn't it know us more than we know ourselves?

        I can feel a tree growing inside, thrusting its way outwards.

Are we all just trees, our thoughts and senses roots and branches?

        What's your favourite word?

Mine is *cleave*.

        It rhymes with Eve.

That's not why it's my favourite word, it just occurred to me.

        We all cleave to something.

A coot cleaves the smooth water.

The unassailable Percival cleaves through the ranks.

It's the consonant I'm particularly fond of. The way it splits into the liquid *L* then eases itself through the *EE* passage before becoming subsumed at last into the fractured, almost fricative *V*.

A separation and a binding.
Words have their own world-making beauty and terror, their own anthropology, archeology, music and myth.

We live inside our mother's tongue.

We are knotted to her principles.

Now that I pick out the *V* it makes me think of...

What does it make you think of?

A shell? A mouth?
A snake's tongue?
An arch? A cave?
A root? A tunnel?

The Threshold.

§

The words are looking through you.

Clairenvoi

I remember nothing   but a mirror I
know it is a mirror   because it hangs on
the opposite wall   and when I stand in
front of it   a figure looks back and
moves as I move   and looks through
me as I look into it   but then it opens
like a door and I pass   through it. I am
walking inside what I   thought was a
mirror   but
is in fact a   cupboard door. I am
standing inside behind   the mirror. I turn
around so I am facing   the back of the
mirror. I hear footsteps   outside, they grow
in size, then stop.   They too must be
looking in the mirror now.   They are
looking in the mirror at themselves   in the
mirror with me looking back behind   the
mirror. They walk forwards, I walk back.

    The door opens and they come inside
    the mirror. I feel their tired breath on
me.   I squint to find their eyes, but there is
no   light, only the smell of must. I feel
about for   the dark corners, but my legs
give way, only   it is not my legs, it is the
floor beneath.   I am free-falling from a
terrible height.   There is a faint light
that is growing   as I fall, the wind
rushes past, the dark air   grows thick as it
slides into me.   I find it hard   to breathe. I
see a hand holding a light and   attached to
the hand is a long arm and   attached   to
the long arm is a torso   and attached to
the torso is a neck and a head.   The head
gets bigger and bigger and then   I see a
whole figure is standing inside the mirror.
It is dark, very dark, but the deeper I look into
it,   the more I see and the less I fall.

Very soon I will open my mouth

and say something

say something

something

say

something

say   something

something

something

something

something

something

something

something

something

something

something

2

Time of Milk / Stay-Home Time

Portobellologue

~How long have I been hidden away like this?

~Are you hidden? Hidden from what?

~I've been sitting in this little box for so long, no one has come.

~That's not true.

~The world is invisible to me.

~You have visitors.

~Like who?

~Me!

~You can hardly call yourself a visitor.

~What am I then? Would you like me to go?

~No.

~I'll tell you a story. Once upon a time...

~Not that one.

~Yesterday I was over by the bridge.

~No!

~Today as I was walking by the canal...

~What's that one?

~A new one.

~Have you told it before?

~Never.

~Where did you get it?

~I heard it from a stranger.

~When?

~Not long ago. Would you like me to tell you one you know? I'll start again. Today as I was along Portobello I stopped into the arcade and bought something...

~Bought what? Be specific.

~I bought a spade.

      ~A spade from the arcade?

~Why not?

      ~I don't buy it.

~Well, I did. The ace of spades.

      ~The card?

~Yes.

      ~Cards don't come singly. They live in packs.

~Live? Shall I continue?

      ~No.

~Would you like me to go?

      ~Just stop talking.

~If I stop talking how will you know I'm here?

Yoga for Beginners

Mountain

Stand up straight. Feel your weight evenly balanced through the base of each foot. Bring the feet together. Lift up the toes. Spread them wide and place them back on the floor. Stay in the present. Not leaning back. Not leaning forward

Tree

Shift weight onto right leg. Sole of left foot inside right thigh. Hips forward. Prayer. Arms over shoulders. Focus on a moment. No. A particular object of desire. No. An object in front of your eyes. Anything that sits dumb. A specific inanimate object. The green succulent by the window that lives almost entirely without water. Hold. To be self contained. A vessel. To not drain. Unless. Breathe. Bring control. Repeat on the other side

Headstand

Bring the crown of the head flat to the floor. Settle brittle, bitter, cold. Lift the right knee. Clasp elbows. No. Make a fist. Walk the toes in. Head crowning. Strike a balance, breathe. I love the sound of music. Not the musical, I mean the actual *sound* of music, the sound of it. I think music has a certain sound that when you hear it, well, it's like love isn't it. Phlegmatic. Pragmatic. Strike a balance, breathe. Do they see her when they see me? Control save

Happy Baby

Once upon a time the woodsman paid regular visits to the mother when the father was out; was it the woodsman or the milkman? Bring the arms through the insides of the knees. It sounded like she was being milked like a cow. Tuck the chin into the chest with the head on the floor. The woodsman came to visit the daughter one or two times. Press the sacrum and tailbone down into the floor. He took a great interest in her teeth. *You have a very fine rack.* He was obsessed with oral hygiene. He asked her to open her mouth. Said it was clean as a cat's, and that he could see the universe. Pull back. He gave her something to put in it and told her she was a good girl. Pull back. One day the mother came in and found blood on the sheets, or was it milk? They didn't cry. Let the legs open wider. Breathe and hold for 4-8 breaths

Child

Lower the hips to the heels and forehead to the floor. A man in the bookshop asked me if I had Aristotle's *Poetics*, I told him I didn't work there, he said he was aware of that and asked the question again. I gave him a blank stare. Have the knees together or, if more comfortable, spread the child and knees slightly apart. I said I should like to read all the books in the world, but my mother said when you've read one you've read them all. This is the way it is. Breathe deeply, actively pressing the belly against the thighs on the inhale. When you breathe out feel all the stress leaving your body blank

Slumped

What is said out loud and what remains repeated in the head? Relax wrist .pucker lips .release filter-tip and place between teeth .and light .inhale .hold .close your eyes shoulders relaxed *sho-ping* Hold exhale relax belly inhale slight draught ache in knee .Hold .feeling queasy after ...*shop-ing* .milk eggs bread fish exhale must ring Susan *sho-ping shop-ing* inhale and hold .feel yourself go deeper down the dark must keep going soldier on exhale .I heard the same noise last night I got out of bed .nothing stirred everything sleeps .this is what it all comes down to .a hesitant blip that whirs in the chest pocket .an affirmative text .a weekend of rain *shop-ing* .a tweet of a bird with a stop in its throat .inhale .there are more Barbie dolls in Italy than there are Canadians in Canada .Fact .in the next 60 seconds you have the chance to win 60.000 dollars .Like .water is the most common found substance on earth .Wow .breaking news :another child washed ashore .you're trying hard to find something to say .Sad .Anger .exhale .you find a man standing alone by a door and accost him but it all comes out Italian .hold .he stands by the blinds .inhale .now he is a cat .inhale a cat on its hind legs picking off flies from the window .hold .I go up to him and start stroking his back, now he is licking my hand, then my face .he is eating my face! *Reeeooooaaaaraurauroooaauurauuuoooooooorauraurauraurraaaaaauarhhhh!* Imagine a sky .that is the mind .this is my mind .this is my thought .this is my heart .this is my room .breathe

Eagle

Phlegmatic pragmatic strike a balance breathe .do they see her when they see me ?feel yourself drowning under every word .focus feel the cord coming out of the crown .legs grounding into the floor place the hands on the bent knee .breathe .let go so as to be as we are into the next room .hold this then now .over and again .strike a balance breathe .straighten the arms to draw the torso back .horns of people in black shiny clothes filling the roads .burgers and petrol lager and crisps patchouli and hash piss and chips .they duck down a lock and hold shoulders down and draw the blades towards the spine .two strangers become a foreign body lift your chest .muddy water swirling tin cans .these are his hands .trolleys lank limbs .silvering slivering .this is his chin .two strangers come .breathe .How many years ?The whole city looking the other way .this is his ear gasping for air .and breathe and hold .this is your torso .this is your core .sinking into the flesh .shit trolleys limbs of the dead .breathe .this is your head .the bitch river getting her way .gulping for air .until .hold. The cord broke

Corpse

And then what ?the same amount of water on earth as there was when the earth was formed .repeat .more people alive today than have ever died .the water from your faucet contains molecules Neanderthals drank ...And then nothing .breathe again .no sun no moon no matter .black hole .frog in my throat .cat in the flap .bit of a chip stuck in my larynx .nail .used condom .down the plughole .nothing at all .hands close .their warm grip .a comfort and a thief .unlike the others .frame much slighter .what do we do what do we say when ?This is the way it is .he disappeared one winter with my tongue nobody spoke his name I have no idea what became .perhaps all life is nothing but a titter and a lick .there are so many books in the shop it's impossible to know which one is for me .what ails thee ?I've been holding a very small part of you but where is the rest ?your body your arms your legs ?you're a figure of speech .two truths :one under .the other is over

Lotus

Close the eyes and rest .and now the same room .and then the eye of the fingers the mind of the flesh .and touch and flex .a room that is full and empty .and fill and fall .Love Mother Steeple Church .People Father Sever Hold .Apple Ripple Able All ...and then ...and then ...and them ...and then ...and then ...and them ...and then

.Hold

3

Bright Fire / Shoots Show

The Wrongs & Rites of Grosvenor Square

Speak to me, son.
Thou hast affected the fine strains of honor
To imitate the graces of the gods,
To tear with thunder the wide cheeks o' th' air
And yet to charge thy sulfur with a bolt
That should but rive an oak. Why dost not speak?
Think'st thou it honorable for a noble man
Still to remember wrongs? — Daughter, speak you.

from *Coriolanus*, William Shakespeare

The time is the place, which is Grosvenor Square, Rathmines, Dublin 6. Two front adjacent lawns. Hot, humid day. Hazy sunshine creates strange pale light, as if of an eclipse. A couple, Stephen and Medbh, are painting their black wrought iron fence. Next door, a nameless neighbour, sits on a bench in her garden intermittently writing in a notepad. Stephen has earplugs in; he is listening to a game of cricket. Silence as they paint. Sounds of birds, tennis and bowls on the square. A siren wails from the nearby barracks, followed by church bells.

Medbh is distracted. After some time, she makes a call on her mobile.

Medbh Aisling? What's going on? Can you hear me? No, I can't... He's working. Where are you...? What? You're breaking up. No, he's listening to a game... Aisling are you listening to me? Talk to me.

Medbh hangs up.

(To Stephen.) That was Aisling... I said that was... *(Medbh notices the writer writing.)*

It looks like it might break... The weather.

Look at the sky... The sun is so strange. It's like a dirty window.

Stephen What did you say?

Medbh I said... do you not find it close?

Stephen *(Mishearing)* It's over there.

Medbh Look at the sun. It's like a white fire.

Stephen Don't be looking too long. You'll ruin your eyes.

Stephen and Medbh continue to paint.

Medbh Stephen, watch out. We don't want black roses.

Stephen I'll open another tin.

Medbh Don't shake it... Stephen, don't shake it. *(Stephen starts to shake the tin.)* Stephen!

Stephen Did you say don't shake it?

Medbh Not that one. Stir it, lightly. Do you want me to do it? Read the tin. I'll stir it.

Medbh's mobile rings. Medbh answers. The writer appears to be listening and writing.

Hi, Niamh... Oh we're fine. We decided to paint the railings for the day that's in it. No we're fine. Very close... Yes. It's the same here. Like this for the weekend... She would have done, yes. Thank you for, calling. *(To Stephen)* Just a light stir. It's Stephen... OK. Bye, byebyebyebyebyebyebye.

Stephen Who's that?

Medbh Niamh.

Stephen *(Under his breath)* Christ!

Medbh She means well. At least she remembered.

Stephen And she needs to remind us. I thought you were going to deadhead those bleeding hearts?

Medbh Of all the days.

Stephen They're done for.

Medbh *(Towards the writer)* It looks like it might break... *(To Stephen.)* I think she's writing what we're saying.

Stephen What, I'm not saying anything.

Medbh Watch this. *(Medbh exaggerates)* Yes I'm afraid she's gone and done it again, she goes through them like water, she's in pieces. I told her to pull herself together. She won't listen.

Stephen Who are you talking to?

Medbh No one.

Stephen First sign of madness... Oh no. Oh damn, damn, DAMN.

Medbh What?

Stephen Bell! He's out.

Medbh She's writing what we're saying.

Stephen Who is?

Medbh She is. A writer.

Stephen How do you know?

Medbh She's very pale. Look... *(Exaggerates)* Look at the sky. Stephen!

Stephen What?

Medbh Look. It's like a girl in a billowing dress swirling around.

Stephen What are you talking about?

Medbh It's a daffodil opening.

Stephen You'll go blind.

Medbh It's like a simmering pot with the lid rattling off.

No, it's a pill, dissolving in water... Look!

Stephen What is it?

Medbh She is writing.

Stephen You shouldn't stare.

Medbh She's like the moon...

Stephen You shouldn't stare!

Medbh It's a test.

Stephen The Test? Bell is out.

Silence.

Medbh You're a writer, I see. Nice day to write. Do you write much?

Writer A bit.

Pause.

Medbh The sun is so dark.

Writer Hmm?

Medbh The light, strange, wouldn't you say? It's like looking through a tunnel. There's no power to the sun and yet it feels so close... What are you writing?

Writer Now.

Medbh What?

Writer Nothing.

Medbh Nothing? And you'll keep working on it will you... I mean until you have something, concrete?

Writer Perhaps.

Medbh It's like a tomb, the sun, or a soft womb.... *(Under her breath)* Soft... That reminds me of my boss... yes, that's right, the other day, I said Mr. Samson are you having a joke with me and he said, 'Why would I be having a joke. I asked you to take them off.' I had to, or he led me to believe I had to... he wasn't wearing his, no. I took them off and entered.

I could see why he had his off, it was comforting to feel the shag pile under stockings... quite a different sensation to the one I was used to in the office, with its wooden edges and metallic lines. To feel the softness brought out something else. I felt quite at home, something I've never felt in an office before.

I didn't always paint railings. In my salad days I could walk down long roads and wide avenues, my life opening up. I didn't know what anything meant, or what I stood for, and yet I was opening. I'd no idea what would happen to me, just as I'd no idea what would be waiting for me at the end of the road. Then I caught a man looking at me on the other side as I crossed, I turned to catch his eye, and at that moment a car screeched its brakes and stopped inches from where I stood. I could have died right there in the middle of the road, standing for nothing, utterly meaningless.

But instead I fell in love.

Another man in the office asked me if I had children. They're all very curious about my home life. They must wonder what I'm like outside the office. Well it's what you do isn't it; you imagine what people are like. When I buzz people through, I only hear their voices, but sometimes I get a vivid sense of what they are really like, a snap-shot of what kind of rug and furnishings they have at home, what kind of husbands or wives they have, but I never think about children, yet that's all the men seem to think about, their phones are full of children.

It's my secretarial skills that have kept this house afloat.

I sometimes wonder what would have happened if the car had knocked me dead. I wouldn't be here watching him paint roses black, up to our knees in weeds deadheading bleeding hearts.

These damn flying ants... we're being invaded....

Medbh takes out her mobile.

Aisling. No I can't. I know it's dark, it's dark here too. If I could come and get you I would, you understand that don't you? Look at the sky, can you see the sun? Of course there is, look harder... Aisling? Aisling? What's wrong? What are you saying?

Stephen Who was that?

Medbh What?

Stephen Who you were talking to?

Medbh I couldn't hear anything she was saying.

Stephen What?

Medbh I said... oh it doesn't matter.

Stephen Look! The clouds, they're rushing out so fast.

Medbh I told you. This square is moving in circles.

(To the writer) I could come and take it from you? I could rip that page from its spine and screw it in a ball and put it in my mouth and swallow it.

I'm going to!

Medbh, fatigued, retreats indoors.

Silence as Stephen paints railings.

Stephen Always great to give the bars of the cage a lick of paint.

He considers the writer and starts talking in the blind hope of striking up a conversation.

You'll have to forgive her. She hasn't been the same... You're a writer aren't you? These railings date back to the 1880s. Some people would like to replace them but they can't, they're of historical significance to the square. A lot of people wonder... Lots of people wonder... why the architecture on this square is so varied.

He pauses, hoping for a reply from the writer.

The writer starts to write.

It's because they were built at different phases for the British army... the HQ was just across there. It's a barracks now. Christ, look at that cloud.

They were built for different ranks. That's why you see high-ceilinged, tall window houses like ours... then over there you have the smaller, short window houses. The higher you ranked, the higher your ceilings, you see, and the higher your ceilings the taller your windows. Taller windows mean more light.

You're a writer. My daughter used to scribble. A few famous artists lived here. George Russell, painter, poet, mystic, educated at the local school, and there was the folklorist, mythologist thingamy-poet Ella Young who lived just there... she was famous for dressing in flowing purple robes, fancied herself as some latter day druid I expect – *ha!* She was part of... what do you call them... the revivalists Yeats, Lady Gregory, that whole set up. They read at Rathmines Town Hall, where the clock is, the four-faced liar.

Each side still tells a different time.

Then of course there's Bram Stoker, he lived a few doors down, the one with the red door.... he even composed a little known poem called 'The Wrongs of Grosvenor Square', based on the topical issue of the day which was omnibuses passing through, disturbing residents on the square. That's why we have those bollards on one end to stop traffic passing through and disturbing the peace. (These damn ants.) It's all thanks to Stoker's poem. (Look at them sticking to the railings, what a way to end.) Not that it's a terribly good poem. Aren't you a writer? (All this paint will seep into the ground if it rains. It's getting darker.) It was the first time Stoker tried out other dialects, which of course he used more famously in his better-known and ground-breaking, Dracula. Other than that, it's not a terribly good poem.

I'll tell you why I think it's not a terribly good poem, because Bram Stoker was not a terribly good poet. The odds in that regard were stacked against him from the start. Nevertheless he gave it a go and no doubt had it published in the *Telegraph* or the *Times* and it titillated a few of its readers and even went some way to the present bollards which stop passing traffic. So I suppose it did make something happen, even if it was a bad poem. That's why he became a novelist. You're a writer. All novelists are failed poets. Even the novelists who claim to hate poetry are especially failed, as their denial is so deep.

Look at these roses. Have a whiff.

The writer looks up as if about to say something... but doesn't, she simply reflects and stays blank.

Sounds of bowls from the square.

How sweet life is before it dies.

It wasn't always bowls and tennis on the square. It was originally a cricket green. I'm listening to it now. I can hear the bat thwacking the ball out of the air.

Smell this rose.

The writer stands up and walks towards Stephen.

They stand opposite each other, the bordering railings and roses between them.

Stephen plucks a rose head.

They look at each other, something crosses between, and that something is an animal.

Stephen then drops the head into the flowerbed.

Rotten rose of all my woes.

Stephen draws back.

We had a girl who lived with us for a while, she wrote poetry, again not terribly well but she cut her teeth with it, studied her craft. She went away, because Medbh – that's my wife – Medbh, my wife, couldn't stand to look at her face any more. She couldn't bear her own flesh and blood standing above us beating out iambic pentameters each night. You could hear her booming blank verse through the chimney. Anyway Medbh hates her now, or perhaps she's just averse to her verse – *Ha!*

She doesn't have the patience or time that poetry requires, you see. You're a writer. She also finds the very idea of contemplating a few words on a page as perverse. She calls poetry, and the crooks that write it, subversive. She sees the act of poetry tantamount to treason, a kind of act against the state. So it's just as well you don't write poetry or she'd bring back the British army to drag you out and court-martial you.

The writer sits down. Distant sounds of thunder rumbling to itself.

For a start, she says – this is her not me – she finds it deeply dispiriting how poets don't write to the end of the line, leaving all that blank space. She hates waste. I mean in Japan she read, in Japan it's said they write poems that are just three lines long – three *fecking* lines – with only a few words in each line. That, she thinks, is what led to the kamikazes, finishing themselves off mid-flight, mid-sentence as it were. Not to mention finishing many others off in the same token. What a waste! The poor readers who have to make sense of it though. – she says, not me. So that's why she abhors poems, or poets possibly, most probably both.

Listen, can I say something to you? Last night I couldn't sleep. All I could hear was her indoors snoring, and in the snoring I heard a little girl crying, and inside the little girl, a baby wailing. Inside the baby was a clock, repeating the same phrase over and over, talking to itself. It didn't want to forget what it had just thought, so it thought if it repeated it like a mantra, it would stay with it, over and over.

What then can happen I thought, is a continuation of a thought from a very long time ago... a thought years past remaining frozen in the shadows of a place then unlocked at any moment in some forgotten future.

Writer mouths Stephen's following lines as he speaks.

Then, out of nothing, words take over. Despite the rigour of grammar, pure language pours out and floods everything we know.

A language writing us.

We want to exist always in this endless stillness.

Shadow ends. Applause from the bowls green. Stillness.

The writer looks out with a speaking-silence of the Mona Lisa.

Stephen I mean look at you sitting there, milk-white like a salt pillar, or a stone gone cold. You're complete aren't you, recording everything. All your thoughts, all my thoughts. All of this. Together.

Look at that cloud. That storm's really not far.

We had a daughter. She used to write. She'd never be apart from her pen and pad. We were in the garden painting the railings when we got the call. She phoned in the middle of the road just after it happened.

There was no ceremony. We decided against it. None of the tizz of last offices... no song, and certainly no eulogy.

But I remember the wind rustling the leaves like a tramp sifting through rubbish, repeating the same words without meaning. Pure thought.

A wind of things that can never be pinned down.

She was never quite herself, never quite settled, always turning things over like a filthy tramp.

After everything, what is there? The tide covers the prints in the sand.

I can't even be sure anymore she was ever here... now... then...

perhaps...

(In a low voice, under his breath) The world within a word... unable to speak.

Silence.

The writer looks down and starts writing.

What she writes we do not know, nevertheless she writes, blackening the paper with words so there is no difference between text and margin.

A wind picks up.

Stephen becomes increasingly agitated.

I've got to stop you there because you are actually completely wrong. You're completely and utterly incorrect in everything you say. You're completely and utterly out of line. You're a writer. I don't think you've listened to a word I've said. I don't think you're listening to what I'm saying. No, I think you've assumed what I'm saying before I've even said it. You've followed a thread of your own thinking and tuned out of anything I've said. I've been wasting my breath, talking into a vacuum... I might as well have said nothing, I've said less than nothing, because you've come up with something else entirely – from what I haven't said – for your own slanderous slant.

A peal of thunder rolls and hovers like a rose of impetuous beauty.

You know I get mixed up sometimes. Stoker's poem was based in London, it wasn't this square at all; it has nothing to do with the bollards here. I'm not even sure he lived here.

We're a long way from that Grosvenor Square.

History is wrong. We fill it with our own shite. Yesterday's revelation is tomorrow's deception.

She gets very mixed up. You mustn't be angry that she doesn't see. She gets so tired now. But you never seem to tire. You're always there, always... like a statue, or Stoker's poem.

I'll tell you another thing about writers. They're always thinking about something else all of the time; they're never in the present. I mean when anything happens, instead of actually just experiencing the moment they immediately start playing it over in their head and considering it as potential material for their next work. They're never just experiencing a moment as it is, they're constantly turning reality into something else.

I mean, take the sun. If her upstairs in that dead house were to take it, she'd say, 'It's the eye of a storm.' Or, 'An eye of truth amid a whirl of chaos.' Or she'd write – this is her not me – 'It's like a cup of hot steaming truth.' Or, 'The child of goodness.'

All you see, I suppose, is a sundial by moonlight telling the wrong time. One day the sun will be as cold as the moon, she said.

Numinous goddess in luminous stone numinous goddess in luminous stone.
A milk-white transience – a milk-white transience –
transparent as net curtains transparent as net curtains.
A stony silence afloat in infinite space a stony silence afloat in infinite space.
And all the roses return to a tight-lipped black and all the roses return to a tight-lipped black.

Wedding bells ring out.   *A marriage of opposites.*

Christ! When it comes down to it they are like parasites poets, draining the teat of the state, feeding on human excrement, they suck every idea dry until there's nothing left! They take all the sweetness out of the rose and stuff it up their stuffy noses, stealing the smell, taking the life. That's why roses smell of nothing now. A blind hum.

(Shouting) You've destroyed all our roses!

The black is getting into everything. I should paint you black like a railing, or a rose that's been burned alive.

Our blank statue, forever standing for nothing in our garden.

I mean when you actually think about a bunch of people with pens writing lines that may not reach the end, or even get close to the bottom of the page while at the same time turning every experience into material they should be rounded up in my opinion. Ah, these flying fucking ants!

A flash of lightning, a crack of thunder.

The wind blows harder.

Slow fade on Stephen.

Light brightens on the writer.

Medbh runs out with her mobile.

Medbh Stephen!

Stephen What is it?

Medbh It's so bright. *(On her mobile)* Aisling, what are you saying? Speak to me... What are you saying?

Stephen *(Snatching the mobile)* Aisling?... *(Listening. His tone softens)* The moon, it's rising... so bright, yes.

Medbh Tell her how everything's just as it is.

Stephen I'm listening to the great game.

Medbh Tell her how everything glows, that we've kept everything just so. Tell her nothing's changed.

Stephen Bell is plucking the ball out of the air.

Medbh Tell her all the flowers are opening, their fragrances filling the square. Tell her how lucid the mountains look. Tell her about the perfect temperature.

Stephen The railings are jet black, the roses blood red.

Medbh Tell her it's all right, tell her we're not afraid. Tell her she can wear her favourite dress. Tell her nothing's changed. Tell her!

Stephen Nothing's changed Aisling.

Nothing's changed.

Nothing's changed.

Lightning flashes
                              the thunder roars like a great cat.
Darkness descends
        on Medbh and Stephen.

The writer   grows brighter   a heavy downpour approaching.

She rises to the changing moon.

The 'I' of the writer dissolves in the writing
branching off   into various parts.

The myth looks over the shoulder
                        of the writer,
                        the writing
                        and the written.

White noise   becomes overwhelming.

This combination   creates   an invisible architecture   transcending
spatial and aural definition.   The rite of birth
through death   squares the circle.

The end brings out a curious epilogue in which the writer at last becomes the action. The length
of time this position is held is a private contract between performers and audience to be
negotiated internally each time which will inevitably shape and determine the

blankout.

4

Lugh's Wedding Day / Claim Time

Epilogue

This is the way. The way it ends. The way always. This is the way. Always the end. It comes back. This is the way. The way it returns. This is the end. On repeat.

Repeat the one. The one who loves. The way it is. The way it returns to the one who loves too much. It always returns.

This is the way. The way back. Back to the one who can't forget. The way a moment forgets to end. This is everything. This is the end. Return the way it always ends. This is the way. Everything back. It always ends. The same moment.

Time returns. It comes back. Back again. The way it returns to the one who loves too much and can't return the same moment.

The way it begins. On repeat. The same love. The same forget. The can't forget. The can't return. It comes to. The way the way always ends. Back to back. The one who returns the same moment.

Love returns. Everything on. Everything on repeat. Love forgets the way time returns. This is the end.

The same same. The same one. The same time. This is the way time ends. The same love. Return everything. Time again. The way the way is always the way. Time returns. This is the way love forgets the same moment. Love returns to the same end. Back to time. Repeat return. Too much time. Not enough love. Not enough moments repeat the love. Repeat the one who loves too much. Who loves everything to the same end.

Love is the way. No return. The one-way. The way it comes. It comes on. It comes back. It moves in. It backs in. The way it is. Back to back. The same way. The love-back. The one who returns the one who can't love. Love is love. Too much. The same moment. Back to forget. Back it up. The same moment. The same love forgets time. Forget forget. It always returns. Everything back. The way it comes. The way it begins as it returns.

The love time. The love to. The love who. She comes through. Forget time. This is the way it begins. The way it always does. The same love forgets the same moment.

This is everything. The same way. The love way. The always time. The comeback. Love returns to the one who forgets too much and can't remember the time it went back to the same moment. Time repeats the way it begins. The way the way can't return. This is the way it begins to forget. The way it returns time. Love begins. The same moment. The way the way is the way. The way it returns the one who forgets on repeat and can't love back to back the same moment. This is the moment. The moment it ends with the one who forgets love and remembers the way back to everything on repeat. This is the way it begins as time moves as love forgets. It comes to the one who repeats the way it returns the one who loves too much and can't forget the way it went. The same time returns the same moment to the same one who comes back to the way it always begins. The way it will. Love to love. It always does. Always love.

Always.

The way.

Return.

Begin.

On

The Great Friend

In the Autumn of 1244

a young Muslim scholar of Konya
met a new arrival who'd been travelling

throughout the Middle East.

This stranger put a question to the scholar:
it remains one of the great mysteries.

Whatever the question,

the young scholar lost his breath and fainted.
When he came round the two talked and became

locked in a stream of endless dialogue.

Inseparable, they spoke for days without human need –
like two musicians riffing, each one taking over where

the other left off in a state of pure discovery.

Late one night, mid-discussion,
the friend went to attend a knock at the door

and didn't come back.

The young scholar fell silent and vowed never
to speak again unless his great friend returned.

He had fallen into what is known

as the deep well of meditation, the narrow
tunnel of mortal contemplation.

For months, not a word passed his lips.

Then on his darkest night he looked up
and let out a savage howl. As he screamed

he found a new voice forming.

The next morning, he headed to the market square
and began to speak. Poetry and parables poured out:

You are the sky my spirit circles in.

My soul is from elsewhere. *He started*
to sway and outstretching his arms whirled around,

spinning between food stalls,

weaving teachings out of chickpeas; forming fables
about burnt kebabs. A large crowd gathered,

some started to swoon and dissolve

into laughter, others moaned in ecstasy
and cried. One young man began writing

his every word down.

The Konya scholar had lost all simile
and became the thing itself: the lover, the beggar,

the parched earth, the unfurling flower.

He continued turning into the small hours,
his great friend returning through him.

A mute moon smiling in the wings.

about:blank World Premiere Dublin Theatre Festival 2021.

Experience *about:blank* as an audio-immersive journey at www.aboutblank.ie
Performed by Olwen Fouéré, Paula McGlinchey and Owen Roe.

This digitally downloadable event is available via an interactive website complete
with a built-in algorithm where you are guided through the piece and asked to
listen to it in a self-selected scenography by responding to prompts.

Directed by Eoghan Carrick, this binaural performance comes with an original
score and sound design by Cormac O'Connor and Frieda Freytag.

Funded by the Arts Council Ireland, Abbey Theatre and Poetry Ireland with the
assistance of the Abbey Theatre/Amharclann na Mainistreach. Supported by
Civic Theatre, Mermaid Arts Centre, Museum of Literature Ireland and
Riverbank Arts Centre. Produced by Melissa Nolan.

ADAM WYETH IN ASSOCIATION WITH THE CIVIC THEATRE
AND DUBLIN THEATRE FESTIVAL 2021 PRESENTS

OLWEN FOUÉRÉ   PAULA MCGLINCHEY   OWEN ROE

about:blank
30 Sep - 17 Oct

An online audio-immersive work

Written by ADAM WYETH • Directed by EOGHAN CARRICK

Tickets €11 from www.civictheatre.ie

Funded by the Arts Council, Abbey Theatre and Poetry Ireland
Developed with the assistance of the Abbey Theatre/ Amharclann na Mainistreach
Supported by Civic Theatre, Mermaid Arts Centre, MOLI and Riverbank Arts Centre

Acknowledgements

For this work, I gratefully acknowledge the Arts Council Ireland for the Literature Project Award 2020 and an Abbey Theatre, Engine Room Development fund, towards the audio-immersive production of *about:blank*. My heartfelt thanks go to the whole about:blank team who believed in the project from the start: Olwen Fouéré, Owen Roe, Cormac O'Connor, Eoghan Carrick, Rike Freytag, Melissa Nolan, Paula McGlinchey, Noelle Cooper, Alex Connolly and Ste Murray. A big thank you to all our Creative Partners: Abbey Theatre, The Civic Theatre, Poetry Ireland, Museum of Literature Ireland, The Mermaid Arts Centre and The Riverbank Arts Centre.

Publications
Some extracts of *about:blank* featured previously in the following books and magazines. 'Untitled' published in *Correspondences*, an Anthology, ed. by Jessica Traynor and Stephen Rea (2018). *about:blank* Part 1 extracts, published in *The Long Poem Magazine*, 2020. 'The Great Friend' was published in *The Music of What Happens*, ed. Tanya Farrelly, (2020).

Performances
The Wrongs & Rites of Grosvenor Square had a two-night presentation at the Scene & Heard Festival (2019), Smock Alley, Dublin. Directed by Simon Coury; performed by Paula McGlinchey, John Delaney and Amy Flood. Set design by Alessia Licata.
Yoga For Beginners had a two-night presentation at the Scene & Heard Festival (2017), Smock Alley, Dublin. Directed by Adam Wyeth; performed by Paula McGlinchey.

The four section headings refer to the major Celtic seasonal festivals: Samhain, Imbolc, Bealtaine, Lughnasa, from *The Celtic Shaman* by John Matthews. Lines 28, 29 from 'The Great Friend' are from *The Essential Rumi*, translated by Coleman Barks with John Moyne.

A big thank-you to Noelle Cooper for her input on the blurry line designs and section glyphs.

A special thank you to Jessie and Siobhán for all the tireless work they do at Salmon Poetry – Happy Salmon's Return!

Finally, I would like to extend a very special thank you to those generous readers who offered their encouragement and sharp editorial skills when *about:blank* was at its typescript stage. With a special mention to editor Simon Coury and the punctilious Aifric Mac Aodha; any shortcomings within are my own. My heartfelt thanks also go to Paula McGlinchey, Sarah Hoover, Paul Perry, Annemarie Ní Churreáin, Michael Barker-Caven, Jennifer Brady, James Barnett, John Ablett, Christopher Reid, Keith Payne and Jessica Traynor.

ADAM WYETH is an award-winning and critically acclaimed poet, playwright and essayist with four previous books published with Salmon Poetry. In 2019 he received The Kavanagh Fellowship Award. His debut collection *Silent Music* (2011) was Highly Commended by the Forward Poetry Prize. In 2013 Salmon published his essays *The Hidden World of Poetry: Unravelling Celtic Mythology in Contemporary Irish Poetry*, Foreword by Paula Meehan. His second collection *The Art of Dying* (2016) was an *Irish Times* Book of the Year. Wyeth's plays have been performed across Ireland as well as in New York and Berlin. His play *This Is What Happened* was published by Salmon in 2019. In 2020 he received the Arts Council Ireland Literature Project Award and was selected for the Abbey Theatre Engine Room Development Programme to work on an audio production of *about:blank*. In 2021 he was a recipient of the Live Music & Performance Scheme for *there will be no silence*, a new music and text work, in collaboration with Emmy-nominated composer David Downes, performed by pianist Rolf Hind and cellist Adrian Mantu, with actors Aisling O'Sullivan and Owen Roe, produced by Pauline Ashwood. In 2021 Wyeth was selected for artist residencies at the Heinrich Böll Cottage and the Ámeto Mítico Residency along the Camino de Santiago. Wyeth lives in Dublin where he works as a freelance writer and teaches online creative writing correspondence courses at adamwyeth.com and Fishpublishing.com. He is an Associate Artist of the Civic Theatre, Dublin, and works on ideas and research for the RTÉ Poetry Programme.

Photo: Ste Murray

salmonpoetry40
Cliffs of Moher, County Clare, Ireland